WHY
NOT?

WHY NOT?

BY DAYTON ALLEN

INTRODUCED BY STEVE ALLEN

Illustrated by Tom Zib

PUBLISHED BY
BELLMEADOWS PRESS
WITH
BERNARD GEIS ASSOCIATES
DISTRIBUTED BY RANDOM HOUSE

DEDICATION

This book is dedicated to the two women closest to me, my lovely devoted and ever so helpful editor, my wife . . . what's her name? And to my wonderful . . . what do you call it? . . . that gave birth to me.

—DAYTON ALLEN

INTRODUCTION

By STEVE ALLEN

THE last time I saw Jack Kerouac was late one night in Hollywood last winter. We had just left a recording studio on Sunset Boulevard near CBS and our farewells, for no particular reason, had turned to horse-play. Two days earlier, Jack had appeared on my television show, reading great rolling period-shy paragraphs from his novel "On The Road." Now, in a whimsical mood, slightly intoxicated, he stood on Sunset Boulevard, shouting mildly-obscene pleasantries after me as I walked down the quiet side street where my car was parked, waving good-bye and responding somewhat less raucously not because I have any better sense than he but because I was sober.

The reason I bring this up now is that Jack was not speaking to me in his own voice; he was imitating Dayton Allen. "Steve *Allen*," he was

shouting, at half past midnight, "how's your sister? And Whoy . . . *not?*"

Some may attribute to the power of television,
the fact that Dayton's rubbery-mouthed phrase
"Why not," is now a seemingly permanent part
of the national vernacular, but a moment's
thought will suffice to suggest that very little
of the torrent of wordage with which TV daily
floods the country ever catches in the memory.
The primary reason we remember and are amused
by *Why Not* is that we remember and are amused
by Dayton Allen.

And the "we" I employ is not, I assure you, the
editorial. I personally, and all of the members of
our TV-gang (Louie Nye, Don Knotts, Gabe Dell,
Pat Harrington, Jr. and Bill Dana) are readily
convulsed by Dayton who, aware of our admira-
tion, never fails to respond with an impromptu
show when the opportunity presents itself.

There are not many comedians of his type, and
in any event they are a vanishing tribe. He is
actually an anomaly in the age of the comedy our
show has always presented, and the comedy of
Sid Ceasar, Mort Sahl, Lenny Bruce, Mike Nichols
and Elaine May, Bob Newhart and the other
modernists. Dayton is a throw-back to—well, to

exactly what I'm not sure—but he's a good old-fashioned *nut* and, as George Gobel says, you can't hardly find them no more.

To begin with, he has the *face* of a nut, and that's tremendously important. Fred Allen, for example, for all his brilliance, could never have been a clown-comedian. He wasn't physically the type. But Dayton has a wonderful face for comedy. He is funny just standing there, as the saying goes.

At our rehearsals we frequently would, at odd moments, surround him and begin plying him with questions, to which he would respond as if he were an important personage submitting to a press-conference. His answers . . . wildly inventive, weird, and sometimes for-adults-only . . . were invariably amusing. His range of characters, too, is wider than our television audiences ever knew, for on our show he always played the *Why Not Man,* but he also does fantastic imitations of Eisenhower, Roosevelt, an evil old 19th century cockney inn-keeper, a sort of good-natured village-dope, and assorted Italians, Jews, Negroes, Scotsmen, Irishmen and what-have-you.

This versatility served him well for the many years that he contributed myriad off-camera voices to the old "Howdy-Doody" program, something small-fry viewers are always astounded to learn.

Another thing marking Dayton (who, by the way, is no relation . . . at least not of mine) from other comedians is that he writes a great deal of his own material. Originally his monologues on the TV show were produced by our writing staff, but when they saw what Dayton did with the material, often rewriting it almost completely, they at last turned the full assignment over to him. And, in a day when most books by show-business personalities are ghost-written, it is perhaps appropriate to point out that this one is not. Dayton is a true humorist, as well as a comedian, and this volume proves the fact.

And, like all comedians, he has his serious side. (How could any human—comedian or not—*not* have a serious side?) He invests judiciously in the gold market and gives sober thought to pressing social questions. It is also possible to carry on a perfectly serious conversation with him, at least for a few minutes at a time. But inevitably his rich, comic gift bubbles up into the dialogue, sometimes obliquely and irrelevantly, sometimes as pertinent punctuation to a point seriously intended.

There is not a solitary grave word, however, in this book. For sheer crackling silliness it has something of the flavor of Perelman or Benchley in their very wildest moments. But it is an original, not a carbon copy. Dayton has his own formulas, his own techniques and he uses them brilliantly to strike the magic spark of laughter.

If you're not chuckling aloud by page three, check your pulse immediately: you may be in a bad way.

CONTENTS

WHY
NOT?

chapter one?

NATIONAL SURGEON WEEK

BEING A VERY famous surgeon, surgery to me is more than just a way to make a good fast buck.

A patient and a doctor are two separate people. The patient is one and the doctor is the other. This makes two.

The technical advances in operating have been really swell—clean gloves, nice lights and a bunch of other stuff.

There are certain unwritten laws in surgeon work. Like:

1. Don't get cute. Always wait for the patient to get a little dopey, so they don't feel anything.

2. Before operating, always wash your hands, if they're very dirty.
3. The patient requiring immediate surgery should be considered as sick, and the surgeon shouldn't even kid around.

Quite often, as chief surgeon of the hospital, I would even operate on *people*. Many of these people at the time were even sick.

Of course, once in a while, as in any other profession, you would get a kvetch, which means "crank" in Latin. They would insist I operate with medical instruments. To these I answered simply but firmly, "What are you—a religious fanatic?"

I shall always be indebted to Dr. Iva Spasm, who was my instructor in bellies and heads. Dr. Spasm introduced me to my first patient, who was a real good sport. May he rest in peace. The patient, who at the time looked terrible, was actually suffering from a very bad thing.

I am proud to say that, although I never went to a real doctor school, I honestly hung around an actual drugstore a lot.

Several times throughout an operation, I will stop, look around the whole room, wink, laugh and punch the patient a little. This, to let the nurses and other doctors know that the patient is still alive.

To return to a less comical subject, when I first went into business to do doctor things, I turned away two hundred sick people who came to my office. I didn't want to catch anything. Today, these same people still respect me for this and go to other doctors.

A dear friend of mine, who had been a total stranger to me before I knew him, confided in me and told me an important fact.

Another amusing incident happened when I first started operating. A patient called up excitedly and said he had acute appendicitis and wanted me to please operate immediately. I laughed and hung up on him. I just felt like being silly.

A number of doctors, other than myself, wrote to me, by letter, asking what I thought about a

very terrible disease. I told them, point blank, I thought it was a rotten thing, and was causing the people who had this disease a lot of sickness. To me such truth in medicine is a beacon to the ill.

Just last week ago, a woman customer of mine asked me what I thought about her losing weight. I told her I thought it seemed like a good way to reduce.

I would like to say in closing to those wishing to become doctors: study medicine and stuff like that, learn about hearts and lungs, and those things. It will come in handy, because education is a good way to learn. Also, take a temperature or two, with some sort of thermometer. Take it from me also, the patient who lives on after the operation is a happier patient, boobie!

chapter
two?

EFFICIENCY EXPERT WORK ISN'T JUST KIDDING AROUND OR SOMETHING

WHILE FOREMAN of an assembly plant for making automobile steering posts, I'd just finished a bunch of seven thousand posts in a new way I had suggested, when we found out that they were just fourteen inches too short for the cars. Some blabbermouth said something about it along the assembly line, where they attach them to the wheels or something, and then my boss found out about it.

He came over to me in a huff about it. I tried to calm him down. I told him the first thing that came to my mind. I said, "What do you think the Dodgers will do?"

He ignored my remark and said, "What are we gonna do with seven thousand steering posts that are fourteen inches too short?"

I said, "Can't we paste a little more on the ends?"

The way he answered me, I was sure we couldn't.

He said, "As foreman, how could you let seven

thousand posts go through without looking in on them every once in a while?"

I said, "Number one, I'm not a busybody, and number two, I've got enough work to do just turning out posts in perfect condition, let alone snooping around to see how long they are."

He got all red in the face and pulled his hair quite a lot, and walked away from me, and I realized it was a waste of time to talk to morons like that about efficient operations.

It was with this in mind that I decided there must be others who also need help in business. That was when I decided to become an efficiency expert. All it takes is a lot of good common sense, and a lot of dopey proverbs like, "A good profit will make you more money than all the tea in China," and "If you think you're smart, you're probably dopey 'cause a lot of dopey people think they're smart, too, and they're not."

As an efficiency expert, I cannot waste any time at all, so I told my secretary never to answer the telephone, unless it was someone important. She said it was sort of hard to tell sometimes, just by looking at the phone, if it was someone important calling up. I answered her with one of my proverbs. I said this one to her, "Don't try to get out of the job just by using some rotten excuse, but instead try to do the job." She remained in my employ and is still in there.

Well, one day, a very big business person called up while I was out of the office, and she didn't answer the phone. I got mad as the devil, because I never did find out who it was, and this was the second time he had called.

I told a lot of my clients, who work in secret things, that if they had phones with private numbers they should give their number to their friends without revealing their privates. Like if you're calling up a person—or even someone in business —tell them you're really somebody else, and tell them to call back some wrong number which you can think up right then and give them. The next time you see them, you ask if they got your call, and if they say no, they didn't, you'll know it was you who called.

After that, I painted a new proverb on the side of the desk: ALWAYS ANSWER YOUR TELEPHONE WHEN IT RINGS, IT MAY BE SOMEONE CALLING.

One business lady, who manufactured other things, asked what I could do to make her production better and cheaper. I told her to improve it and bring down the cost. She said it sounded like a familiar suggestion. I told her it quite pos-

sibly was, because I had just said it, and she probably overheard me during the time I was talking to her.

I went a step further. I gave her a plan which was very nice. I said, "Do you know that one man can do the work of ten men? How, you ask? Simple. Just give this man ten times as much work to do."

She got up and left. She was so stupid. I didn't even tell her a proverb.

A man complained to me that he wasn't getting enough things made in his factory. I sat him down and said I'd be right back. I came back in three minutes. I didn't have to go no place after that, so I sat and talked.

I said: "Let us say it takes two hours at full fast speed to turn out five thousand things, and you want to double that. If the machine is a mechanical-driven kind, just make it go faster. Or maybe you even know someone who makes these very same type things you do, perhaps someone who, like yourself, is in your very own kind of business. Then ask him if he wouldn't mind if you borrowed his machine for two hours to make five thousand things. But try not to let him know what you're making on his machine. If he gets nosey, make it like a joke and when they're all finished take the five thousand things out of his factory, by telling him to go to the phone or something. If you're married, your wife could call him and tell him something about a bazaar or other charity."

These, of course, are time and money savers in any man's book. And they are but a hatful of things I have ready to suggest. No proverb required.

A Mr. A. H. came to see me, and he had a chain of grocery stores and wanted to get my slant on getting his operational system on a cheaper and more easy way of it. I snapped back at him, almost a teeny impatiently, feeling it was really too obvious. I said, "Mr. A. H." (Only I used his entire last name and his first one too.) "Mr. A. H., consolidate your operations. You have forty stores. Operate as a single giant business store. Bring all your stores under one roof. The rent you save on the other thirty-nine stores will knock your eye out."

He said, "That's great, only I'll need a fleet of buses to bring the customers from the closed stores to the one that's open."

I said, "Why worry about them? Think of yourself, you foolish person. They'll go some place else."

Just the other time ago, a man came to me who told me he had a very successful business going for himself for fifteen years, but just in the past fourteen years he had been losing his shirt in it. I asked him what was so successful about that? He said it gave him a sense of security. I told him if more people felt like he did America could care for its young. (It doesn't mean anything, but a lot of people feel close to me when I say it.) I asked him if he ever thought about going into some other business, being that the one he was in left him dead broke. He said, "How can you drop something that you've spent your life building up?"

I said, "There's nothing like logic to stop me in an argument." Then I got up and said, "Let me make a phone call for you."

He said, "Make a phone call for me? I don't know anyone I want to talk to now."

I said, "That may be so, but what about them? They may be thinking of you."

There are important rules in business, which actually aren't any different than the rules in some other business. A lot of people ask me how I became an efficiency expert. I have a stock answer for all of them: "None of your business."

The president of a big bank company called

me during a phone call I was having with him, and asked me if I had any idea how he could increase the number of depositors in the bank. I asked what number he had and he said, one hundred and fifty thousand. I said, "Just double that. Get another hundred and fifty thousand and you'll have twice as many."

He thought that was funny, which told me it wasn't actually what he had in mind. He said he didn't want to give any premiums away and he didn't want to do anything else that would make his bank look like a jerky place.

I thought about it for a while, and suggested a great idea. I told him to make an advertisement that anyone could open an account without a cent and the bank would start off by putting one hundred dollars in their account for luck, like you put a quarter or even ten cents under a pillow when you have a tooth knocked out, or it falls out alone, and then you wake up and find that quarter or ten cents I spoke of under the pillow I also just spoke of. Then when the person tries to take out the hundred dollars, you tell them, "You never put a hundred dollars in this bank, what are you, one of those regular lying crazy crooks?" And you warn them you'll call a cop from on the corner or some place very near by.

The owner of a big bus company for people, that drives them all over the whole place, came

to seek my knowledge on how he could make the very people who ride in these buses "Step to the rear of the bus, please," and not make the buses dirty like a slob thing.

I told him two suggestions: First, that if he wanted to do something like that, he certainly was on the right track in trying to find a solution. Two, that nobody in their right mind could blame him for doing just that. But he wanted even more help about it, so I gave it some thought for a minute, and I told him an idea that was a beaut. I told him to build a partition right behind the bus driver, and then when people go on the bus, they would already be at the rear of the bus, please, and the whole back of the bus would remain very clean all the time.

He got up and said, "I just know I can't be hearing this right."

I told him, quite frankly, "But sir, you sure are."

I hugged him, and told him a short proverb 'cause he had to go away right away. I told him, "No matter how many people crowd on a bus there are always some who don't want to be nice, and go back in the rear, and make it dirty too, so don't be mad or nothing."

So remember this proverb I'll give you for free: "If you're a person who fails at one business job after another, don't worry about it, because a lot of people just like yourself are just plain failures in everything in life."

chapter
three?

WRITING A WHOLE
SWELL BOOK
IS NOT MERELY
A SIMPLE THING

To BE A successful author, you must be called one by somebody. When I first decided to become a very famous author, I couldn't make up my mind whether to write a best seller first or struggle for a week or two.

A very fine book-making man with a beard called me up during a phone conversation I was having with him. He suggested I make my writing understandable to people—by having real pictures

in it. I felt then that it was time to show I knew
the business. I insisted they take all of the photo-
graphs by *camera.*

It was practically Steve Allen who told me as a
friend that if I ever wrote a book I should have it
all printed up. I somehow appreciated that, coming from a man I had only known since our very
first meeting.

Many times when Steve Allen and I sat down
together alone, we would talk—sometimes to each
other—and often right in the middle of our conversation. However, most times we would listen
to what we both had to say if either he or I was

talking. I often thought how friendly it would be if we just sat there and looked. I suggested it one time while we were talking about a very important thing—and Steve must have guessed that I wanted to look right then because he didn't say another word. He just sat and looked at me. I met him half way—I looked right to the middle of where he was looking.

You can't sell a book by yourself. You must have an agent; a man who does the work of a person. My agent, bless him, is worth every cent he can get from me. If I've told him once, I've told him at least a bunch of times, "You've done more for me than I can ever pay you for, so why should I even start?"

The agent brings your book idea and maybe a sample chapter or two to the publisher. If the publisher likes it, you sit down with the publisher, and quickly figure out a way to get that agent I spoke of out of the deal. Then you submit to the publisher some more chapters, and as soon as you notice him beginning to wonder if he was right about giving you an advance payment, you call up that agent, who thought you tried to gyp him out of the deal, and tell him how surprised you are that he didn't come around no more, and how the publisher is getting cute.

Soon this agent is working for you again, and selling the publisher on how good your work is. Now your conscience is clear . . . you're going to continue getting paid. After all the chapters have been turned in, all that's left for you to do is to read the best seller list, and before you know it, you'll know every book on the best seller list. Some of them are sort of nice, even for reading. Now it's time for that agent to really go to work, because you now feel you don't need him no more again, and you have a little kind of a fight with him, like you do with friends right before Christmas, about something he may have said, or other.

You have to make personal appearances in different stores, all-night laundromats, and sign autographs of your very name for a lot of people who probably never saw a name in real writing. By this time you have been interviewed on twenty television shows, four great big newspaper columns, while the publisher gave out eight hundred free books, which by this time you feel were actually really sold, and that you should get a certain lot of money from him.

It aggravates you, and also gets you sore, when he tells you they were given away to stimulate sales. You get so sore, you call your agent who doesn't remember now whether he's still working

for you or not, but rejoins you anyway, because he's been reading all the publicity about you, and believes it because he forgot that he sent it all out about you. You tell him that you know there must have been over one hundred thousand books sold already, because your wife told you she heard a check-out boy at her supermarket say his wife read in a column, that books are selling like crazy.

The agent gets all worked up and says he's willing to forget all the misunderstanding, and as your agent he checks on the sales. He soon loses you as a client again because he found out that the publisher was right and not lying and, after all, you don't need some stupid agent to tell you what you already knew anyway.

In writing a book, many times ideas don't work out just the way you think they're going to work out when you first get started writing on the idea. Sometimes for instance the idea you're working on turns out different and so on. These things happen, as I have just explained. If they do, you don't get sore and say, "Darn it, that idea I thought of didn't work out but instead it turned out different." You just take it like a real swell sport and start to work on another idea that may not turn out different in the end like the other one did.

When I first started to write stuff for this book,

I asked my friend and boss Steve Allen, who is actually responsible for himself, if he thought this book would really be an awful success. He said that that was just about the way he'd put it. I said, "Steve, that's what makes the clock tick." It didn't mean anything, but I didn't want to stand there and answer nothing back to him like a dope. He's got a heart of iron.

As you will see most of my book deals with what I have written in it. And as I often say, "Always remember what the greatest writer of all time said, because he said something really nice."

You should know what you're writing about very much so you shouldn't sound overly stupid. In each chapter I wrote on, I made pretty sure that I had all my facts in my very head and didn't trust to luck. Whenever there was something I couldn't think of I wrote it from memory or made it up. That way there was no chance of a slip-up by guessing at the facts. Being an expert in everything I've ever done or seen, I felt that I wanted to help those who didn't know I was an expert in these things I've done and seen.

As you read through the chapters you will get to know what I know, and maybe someday you may say, "I have read this book."

Each chapter is a whole thing in itself, and even people who have never heard me speak by voice will realize in double quick time that these chapters are all that I have written in this book. My next book may not be as complete, but it will certainly have exactly the same amount of information this book has. I promise you that.

Now you ask yourself, is this book going to be a family type book, or is it something that everyone can read without saying, "Gosh, this book sure don't make you feel like you're in a family way."

I sat down with the editor one day because he said he was tired of standing up. I didn't stay long because I had to go home. It was almost suppertime.

Even though I happen to know everything, I made my writing in the book just everyday talk, not smart science-people kind of talking or anything like that. In other words, a moron could read my book and enjoy it probably even more than a brilliant school or science person. I want the average man in the street to feel that he can understand me as well as the man on the curb, or a man leaning against a building wall. A lot of book-writing people try to get uppity and fill their book with like a wiseguy kind of writing. That's all right for those guys, but I don't think the public wants to know about all those uppity things. I think they would rather hear about sort of medium-clever things, written by a person somewhat like myself. I only bring these things out at this time to let people and others know that whoever wants to read my book, it is entirely written, and all the credit for writing it goes to me.

I made a special effort to make sure that only the swellest stuff in my whole mind went into it. After reading it, you'll know me as well as Al Klepper, Conrad Havey, and one other friend I went to summer camp with one year know me. You'll know that I'm telling the finest truth imaginable. My family, like I suppose yours or even others, have always said I would never amount to anything. So it's like a feather in my head to have done so well in everything I've ever done or seen. As you read what I say in each chapter, you'll know that this isn't just a lot of bull. I don't advise anyone who's jealous easily of anyone's success to read this, because just to know that I'm an expert in all these things could make them so really sore, that it could louse up the whole illusion that this is entertaining.

chapter four?

TO STUDY REAL BRAINS YOU SHOULD TRY TO KEEP A HEAD AT ALL TIMES

ALTHOUGH A WHOLE bunch of progress has been made since early times, like 1492 or maybe even 1364, or all those little in-between years, we brain-repair guys still know very little about the inside of a working head.

Today, in science, its brains more than any other part of the entire head that makes real smart inventions. Some years ago a new cookie-cutter could be invented, for instance, by some average-type moron who got a idea for it. But not

so today. Today, to invent real magic-science
things of today's modern times, it takes a practically whole working brain. Let us see what parts
of the brain are used for different things.

The section near the ear, of course, invents bells
and noisy kinds of stuff. This is not just guesswork
but was found out from actual real tests. The
famous Baldwin vibration test is done by taking
a stick from some nearby place, and beating the
test person's head around the ear. Soon that person whose head it is can then hear ringing and
similar noises. If he likes them, he can remember

the sound, and if he wants to, he can invent some machine or other that will make a sound like he is hearing now. Then others don't have to get their heads beat up near their ears to hear that same sound.

To proceed on. The brain is made up of several parts. The front, the back, the sides, and the bottom. The bottom being actually covered from sight by the collar and neck sticking down from it. Also there are a couple of lobes here and there. The front part works the emotions. Like if you get sore at a person, the front part jumps around or something, and if your emotion makes you get happy, it does some other thing.

I guess I shouldn't talk such technical brain-doctor talk, but when you know what I know, it's hard to talk just sociable about it. In the cases of very weird people, we sometimes operate by surgery. This is called a front-of-the-head kind of operation. Everything is done by real science, and you have a nurse, and a mask on you, I guess so the sick guy can't identify you if you goof. Telling it here, I guess it seems like a pretty hard

thing, but no kidding, it's a cinch.[1] In fact while
I was operating on my first patient, I jiggled the
operating table with my foot a little to make the
nurses think I was scared, but then I laughed it
off. Frankly, the time goes so fast operating I'm
not even aware of what I'm doing.

Another doctor, who hangs around in case of
an occlusion or scalpel or that, usually checks on
the blood count, and the patient's breathing.[2] But
always very casually so as not to worry the nurses.
You know how women are. In cases like this, we
always make the patient get right out of bed after
a serious kind of brain operation.[3] I never asked
why, but I guess that's so they don't get medicine
all over the sheets.

[1] In my chapter on surgeon work, I mentioned briefly
about kidding around during a hernia, or some serious operation. I forget what I said, but read it.

[2] I think I mentioned this in my chapter on expert surgeon
work too. Who knows? I may not have, but give it a little
look see.

[3] I don't think I mentioned this at all in the chapter on
surgeon work, and believe me it wouldn't do you or anyone
else any harm to read it over anyway.

Now back to the other sections of the brain, which I mentioned before. The back, sides and the bottom. They are all crammed together in what we surgeons call the head. I merely tell you the hospital part of psychiatry, even though it may be too hard for the regular citizen to understand, so that you will appreciate the case histories I am going to explain.

In many of our test cases, we test brain things out on dogs or animals. If we want to see what happens when we make a chicken mad, we do whatever makes chickens mad and really sore. We do it for a while and then stop for a second or two, and look into his eyes for something. After such tests are completed we can intelligently tell people not to do this thing to a chicken because it makes them get sore at you. They get over it of course, if you give them some corn or something. A chicken is a kind of a good egg.

We experts in the head-fixing things can tell in a moment, by simply fooling around with a real head, what side and corner of it is used for different things. A tap here, a crack on it there, and we know if the person whose head it is, feels these taps or cracks I just spoke of. We now note that the guy whose head we gave a rather decent

crack, felt the pain. Now we whisper in his ear.
Nothing personal, just maybe a little dopey thing.
A mere answering yell like "Ouch," or something,
after the first severe crack we give the head, is
the tip-off to us guys, that the head is in working
order.

Only volunteers are used for all of this work.
Once we went to a school for very smart children.
We asked for kids who wanted to be science-test-
ing people. Seven of the brightest came down
front. We put a lot of wires on their heads, and
tied them all into a machine that made a lot of
noise when the kids did stuff. We told one child
who was very great in music, to bend forward as
far as he could in the chair. He did, and I told
him to go farther, that I'd catch him if he fell. As
he bent over, I stepped casually away, and he
fell right on his head. I finished the test, and told
him I had crossed my fingers when I told him I'd
catch him. When he fell however, it made a lot
of funny lines on the machine's paper.

Meanwhile, another young lad who was excel-
lent in geometry, was asked to sit straight up in
a chair in another room. I then told him to look
straight ahead and think of a hard thing in geometry. Then I poured two quarts of hot melted wax

over his head. It dried up quickly and reshaped his face, funny. It had nothing to do with the testing machine, but I like the kids to know science isn't all seriousness. A little fun goes a long way.

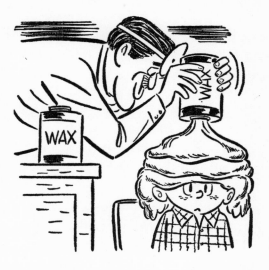

Dr. Robert C. Kitch, a very famous monkey doctor, made a statement in an article he wrote, that changed the whole course of mental business. It's good to have people who think like that in our field, ain't it?

I've treated many rare sicknesses, some of which you hardly ever heard of. I solved all those I cured. One man came to me with a strange problem. His head used to swell up in lumps whenever he had a hard mental problem. I checked into his habits, like if he went to a rough barber or something. I asked him to think about what he might have eaten or done, before these things showed up on his head.

He thought and thought and as he was thinking, he kept banging his head on the desk harder and harder to try to think. He said it made him think better. I removed the inkwell from near where he was thinking, 'cause I just put down a new blotter. Finally he stopped thinking and looked up, and his whole head was like bumpy, and puffed up. He said he really couldn't think of anything. I said I was sorry, I couldn't help him, but I couldn't just guess at something in a case as spooky as that.

When you go to a real head school, you got to attend many lectures and speeches on bodies.

They show you pictures of all naked bodies, with veins, and things painted on them. Nothing dirty.

At one such particular lecture on female bodies, when the talker pointed his stick at the chest area, I started to kid around with a dame doctor sitting in front of me, by putting a couple of oranges I brought for lunch, in my shirt. She got sore, the talking guy got sore, and everybody did, so I cut it out. I merely bring this out to show you how sort of serious they take this.

A woman who had a nervous cough, but was otherwise perfectly healthy, came to me, and asked how she could get rid of it because she felt it was just her mind over matter. I gave her medicine to take which I told her would take her mind off of it, and that way she'd forget it. She came back in a week, and told me that after she took it, her feet swelled five times their normal size, her ears and nose became numb, her stomach was distended, and stuck out in front of her very body, and her heart was giving her trouble for the first time. She also couldn't breathe too good for an hour after each medicine swallowing time, and the cough was deeper than ever. But now this didn't worry her any more, compared to the rest of this junk. I said, "Let's not be a cry baby, and tell me honestly, didn't I get your mind off that nasty little cough?"

We find that a lot of the heads that people have on them, are used for mental purposes. If I may, let me show you how we found this out, if I can get a little spooky with you.

We put five men at a table but gave only four of them a dozen eggs, and one egg box for each of the four. Then we told them they'd have to put them in that egg box I told you we gave to each of them. The fifth man who had no eggs and no egg box, looked around dopey like, and asked where his were. We didn't even answer him. We do many tests like this before we find out something. We feel it's lousy to just guess.

How does the human child feel about his human parents? Many of them like the parents a lot. We did a lot of experimental research on this, and found out that the way a kid feels about his parents depends on how old he is. One time we tried out the Caldwell father-love test. We took a ten-months-old child of the boy sex, and sat him on a chair. We had his father stand a few feet in front of him, and a third larger man came over and punched the father all over his face real hard. The child just looked around and laughed and giggled. I reported that a child of ten months old has no decent father-love, but a swell sense of humor.

I don't know why there's all the worry and stink about teaching kids about sex relations. I did it in two minutes. I said to my son John, "This here is your sister, Mary. She's a girl. This is your brother, Harlow. He's a boy. They are your sex relations, and don't let me hear you say nothing bad or dirty about it."

These things weren't even known to modern brain doctors a thousand years ago. But that's all right, because they didn't know what we know today, so it makes us even. Live and let live.

I spoke on this very subject at some place, just a little while ago, and I got razzed.

As a closing thought, always remember: the best advice you can get . . . . is what you should follow.

A SCHOOL PRINCIPAL JOB
IN A REGULAR
ACTUAL SCHOOL

I HAVE ALWAYS felt that the best way to learn
things is by education, or by gaining knowledge.
I got to be principal of a school quite by accident.
I was attending a large get-together at a big hotel
in a nearby town from where I lived, when I happened to see my town's mayor leaving a hotel
room, with a well-proportioned young lady. I
went up to him and said, "I read in the paper Mr.
Mayor, you went to Mexico for your health. How
do you feel sir?"

He said it had improved suddenly, and what was I doing lately? I told him I wasn't doing as well as he was, and winked a little. I told him I was learning teaching and was delighted to have this opportunity to ask him about a job in the school system when I got graduated. He said he

thought I knew enough right now, and the next day I was made a principal.

When I first accepted my position as principal of my school, I told a group of mothers who came to a school meeting to meet me, "I would do all in my power to learn their kids to be real smart."

As soon as I got underway principalling, I told

the teachers tests were to be given every time, to see if certain individual students were too dumb to get promoted. I prepared a series of tests which I presented to the school board. In it I had questions which, if answered correctly, would tell the teacher if the kid knows the answers in the test. I feel that this way we can best tell how much they know about the stuff in the questions.

You must always be tactful. A parent came to me and said his kid was unhappy because his best friend in his class got gold stars in geography and other school stuff, while his kid stood out in nothing, just because he couldn't learn good like the other guys could. I went over his records quickly, and told him not to feel too badly because he was really head and shoulders over everyone else in stupidity.

I told all the teachers who work in the school place with me, to report to me, youngsters who got real good brains, because sometimes we have children who are smart as anything, and the teacher can't even learn them hardly anything. In our particular school, we classify these students as "Smart as hell." This causes complications in lessons, so I figured a way to eliminate the bottleneck of these youngsters being thrown in with the jerks. I did it by sort of kidding around and telling the more brilliant pupils that they're wrong about what they actually really know, and I make it sound serious 'cause that way they swallow it. Now we don't have no more trouble keeping the smart ones in with the dopier ones.

At a recent meeting of principals of a lot of schools all over the place, I suggested that we make the teachers learn the kids to be smart in more things, so they could face the world prepared to achieve success with dignity, and not just knock their skulls out in some lousy job. So I said, "Let's make them know how to raise penguins, and stuff that every moron doesn't actually get into."

As principal, it is also your duty to maintain a standard of pleasant cheerfulness and niceness. You have to think up proverbs to put on the bulletin boards to make the teachers think they're well paid. I put up such things as:

"A lot of us work for slave wages, but remember, there used to be real slaves, no kidding, and they got beat up a lot too!"

"Isn't it better to be teaching, than be in a chain gang or something?"

"Nowadays a teacher doesn't have to complain about her low wages, because it's taken right out of her salary before she gets it."

A lot of pupils feel that fire drills are not important, so I thought up a way to impress upon them that they were. I called a fire drill one morning, and when they were all outside, I quickly closed my own steel door, and set my own office on fire with a hundred gallons of gasoline. I looked out the window and yelled, "Hey look at me, I'm really on fire!" But nobody heard me, 'cause everybody was already two blocks away in the safety zone. I burned a whole lot of my skin, and a new suit.

Now and then a pupil comes along who really takes all the awards in the school. Such was Harold Klemper. In one term, he took two awards in geography, three in algebra, and all the physical ed. awards in the school. We told his parents, and they made him bring them back and apologize for stealing.

In an election for president of the County Principals' Association, I was placed on the ballot against the only other candidate, a principal who had just been a substitute crossing-guard and former "alky" a week before. I learned that he too had received his position as principal of another school through a city alderman in an experience much the same as I had with his honor, the mayor.

We each made a speech. He apologized for his not being able to speak at this time, because the medicine he was taking to keep from boozing, shrunk up his mouth or something. He got a standing ovation. I didn't know if I could top such sincerity, but I tried.

In essence, I said: "Learning people what to do is what made America a wonderful state. We should make each pupil contribute to this land. Not like contribute a buck for some charity kind of thing, but I mean contribute what's on the inside of their heads. Treat each child like a single person. Try to make the youngster feel that he can even learn from his teacher. This is my ultimate aim, and it's possible, even though this probably sounds like a lot of bull."

The final vote for the presidency of the Principals' Association was based on both our speeches and the opinion they got of us there. It was him or me. On the first ballot, one of us would win, while the other would lose. I lost by a unanimous vote, to the other nice man. It pleased me when they told me, because I felt coming in second was a show of confidence.

Nowadays, juvenile delinquency is a big problem for us principals. Just a short time ago, I was sitting in my office right in the school, minding my own business, when two husky six-year-olds came busting in, and threatened me with their bare fists. I made up my mind to stand up to them then and there. I tightened my lips and said, "Good heavens guys, what do you want? I'll give you anything you ask for."

The tougher one said, "Your nose! That's what we want, your nose!" And he came over and lumped it up a little. I laughed 'cause I knew they'd rather enjoy that, and besides they had more guys waiting outside to see if they really did it to me.

I said, "Well, you sure got it, didn't you?" The weaker one threw an inkwell at me right then.

I believe that good sportsmanship is as important as being fair to each other. Once, a group of third graders came to my office with a little problem. One of the other youngsters had been shaking them down for a quarter a week. I called the boy in and asked him what he meant by that. He explained that he meant to get rich. I told him how unfair it was to take money from the other kids who couldn't afford it. He thought it over for a minute and agreed with me, then pulled a gun out of his pocket and twenty dollars out of mine. I wrote a note to that third grade teacher, not to let those stupid kids pick on this enterprising boy.

Economics plays a large part in how quick kids get smart. Poor pupils seem to get smart on certain things quicker than rich ones. Poor kids learn like almost right away that they can't have anything decent in life. The richer kids who can have all the swell things never get a chance to live in poverty like the poor kids, so it evens up, and each one has something missing in their lives.

I got a note from the school board that the school in which I was doing principalling was having the worst problem with poor attendance in the county. This came just at the time that a lot of kids weren't even showing up in school too. I sent the board back a note that I'd try to do something about it. I spoke at Assembly the next day, and told all the pupils, that if there was some particular problem which I might help solve, regarding their not wanting to go to class, I would be more than helpful to aid them. Then I got talking to them like one of them, so they'd have confidence in me.

I said, "You know, boys and girls, I didn't like school either. In fact I still hate it, but now of course to me, it's a easy buck, and there's a lot of good lookin' young teachers around, so let's try to come to school so you don't louse me up!"

A couple of tough kids in school were brought in to me for cheating on a final examination. I made them stand right in front of me, and tell me the whole thing. They admitted to everything, and I told them I'd have to punish them. I told them I'd have to kick them out of school entirely if they couldn't come up with a good reason why I shouldn't. They said that if I did, their fathers would come down and kick my teeth in. I thought about this threat for a moment, and decided how to handle these punks. I knew I couldn't back down. I went over to them and looked them right in the face, and said, "Now, that sounds like the best reason in the world, so why don't you kids run back to your class and have fun!"

A group of mothers came to my office with a newspaper story saying that our school was the worst-run school in the county. I said, "What's the difference, the kids don't learn nothing here anyway."

I told them I did everything possible to eliminate problems, and make the youngsters want to be smart about things. They said the school was dirty, the teachers were stupid, and the principal was an ignoramus and should be replaced immediately.

I said, "If there's something about the school you don't like, why not bring it to my attention?"

That night I wrote the mayor a letter reminding him how I hoped he didn't get sick and have to go to Mexico again.

chapter
six?

HOW TO BE A NICE FAMILY AND NOT EVEN FIGHT ALL THE TIME

FAMILY PROBLEMS AND marriage fighting could all be overcome, if people just didn't have all that trouble with each other. I find that over the years, almost all of the fights like that, start over an argument of some sort. Why on earth should this be? If people have something on their mind that might start a scene, let them say it even if everyone gets sore.

Nothing holds people together in a family so much as a good taken-care-of house. Children

should feel free to bring in friends if they have to.
You must be proud of the very inside of your
home. One evening, a couple of neighbors of
mine, who just moved in near the corner, came
over and were actually astonished at my home.
They knew I lived there alone, with my wife and
four children, and they asked me how I managed
to keep it looking that way. I told them, with all
proudness, the seven dogs helped keep it looking
in that manner.

They stood up right next to the door all the
time they were there, just looking around quickly,
then at each other. I knew they had never seen a
family living in such a way. The wife of the man
asked if I breeded dogs in the living room. I told
her all I ever did was pet them a little on their
heads. All I breeded was the children.

Their little six-year-old girl was very much
scared of our oldest dog, every time he bit her a
little. I took her aside, and told her a little story
about how kids can get deadly sick from it. The
mother said she never thought anything like this
existed in America. She grabbed her husband and
kids and left. Some people just cannot hide their
envy of their fellow neighbors. I guess it's like
keeping up with the Joneses. That was when I de-

cided that rather than get sore at this stupid jealousy, I should really help people, and so I started my family-helping business.

I tell a lot of my arguing customers how they should be nice, and all that, through real Astrology. I use this with my other smartness about not fighting a lot. I learned Astrology in a whole booklet I read in my dentist's office once.

My first woman customer came to me and told me her husband beat her up every night, and what should she do about it? I asked her if she had a birthdate, 'cause I know women are usually

bashful about that. She said she did, and it was
April 5th, 1923. I asked if she had the date written down somewhere as proof. She said she didn't
but she'd be glad to write it down on a piece of
paper for me. I said that would be fine. Then I
went right over to my old calendars, and looked
it up, and it worked out perfectly. I told her she
was absolutely right—that there really was such
a date. Since that time, I've told many people such
things, but only in very private.

I have many women and children come and ask
me to tell them why they're fighting so much.
Oddly enough, I find the kids born in the past
nine or ten years, are all children under twelve
years of age. A lot of people are embarrassed to
come to a family-helping person like I myself,
especially if you tell them by the Astrology. I tell
them there's nothing to be ashamed of, 'cause
many famous people were born during one of the
months of the year.

One woman came to me quite worried about a
husband of hers who was in a dangerous business
profession, and wanted me to please tell her according to the stars, how he'd make out. I called
my dentist and asked him to look up some page
in that booklet I learned astrology from. I went

back and told her he'd die in three months. She got up all sore or something, and said I was a lot of crap. I told her not to feel that way, 'cause she didn't have to pay me until it happened. I made her promise not to tell her husband, so it would come as a surprise to him.

A woman whose husband was about to make a move to another part of the country, asked if I thought it was right for them to move, as she was pregnant and going to have some kind of a child. I checked on it, and told her she would be terribly happy: her two current daughters would marry rich scientists, and her son would be a famous pianist, and her new child would definitely be a boy. And to top it all, her husband would make her the happiest woman in the world.

She took my advice, and one year later she called, crying that her daughters were carrying on with a drunkard, and a dog murderer. Her son was on dope, and her husband ran off with a charwoman. I said, "What about that new child? Was it a boy?" She said it wasn't. I said, "Well, after all, we can't always be 100 per cent."

Each person's Star Looking-up is different, and it goes by numbers of days. Like if a person is twenty-eight years old, and was born on May 16th of that month, you simply go back twenty eight years of the calendars, and stop on May 16th, and you can tell him each year after that, how old he was.

A man who had been in business a long time and made a lot of money finally got smart, and listened to his wife who told him to see me. I told him he'd lose his business in six months, if he didn't sell it that week. He came back in two years, and said he didn't sell it, and he tripled his business. I said, "What are you gonna prove being a wise guy?"

I stopped telling people how not to fight so much, by using star knowledge, 'cause I don't have any cavities and can't get that astrology learning book in the dentist's office, without looking cheap. Sometimes you have to use common senses.

A mother and father came to me with their daughter and her boy friend, to discuss whether they should get married. They were both still in school, and wouldn't take No for an answer. I told the lad it was ridiculous to think he could take a wife and the attendant responsibilities. I told them both I knew how they must feel about each other, but my conscience wouldn't let me advise two six-year-olds like them, who are still in kin-

dergarten to get married. "So let's be sensible," I said, "and wait a year."

A lot of times I act as a mind helper. Sometimes kids get annoying by crying a lot 'cause they're in severe pain or something. I have often been called in by people who couldn't stand the constant crying or complaining of one or another of their kids. One night while I was doing something I wanted to do, a neighbor called me up about her

child, who was having pains in his face. The
mother recalled that I had told her I specialized
in horsing around to make people forget pains in
the upper left parts of their face.

As soon as I got over to her place, I saw her son
with a hot water bag tied over his face, and tears
streaming down the front of his face from the
pain. His hands were like stretched out, afraid to
move, 'cause the move could make his face hurt
him a awful lot more. I told her that my immediate
opinion of his trouble was, that he was uncom-
fortable. I checked with him on this point, and
he agreed by blinking his eyes slowly, so it
wouldn't move his upper left cheek too much.

I went over and patted his cheek to show I
understood. At this, he seemed to pull away. I
didn't get insulted, because I know kids and kids
don't like to be patted in front of their mothers
or in front of their fathers. The mother asked
what she could do for her son. I told her it was
just a little bit lower than the place I usually specialize in upper cheek pains, but it seemed like the
pain was prethorial bicuspiditis, which to me
meant that the child was teething. She thought
that that might be right too, except that this child
of hers was thirty-three years old. I told her peo-

ple put too much stress on age these days. Ford didn't make his fortune until he was over fifty.

You see, people have all these different kinds of problems, and if some dope got a hold of them, and gave them the wrong advice, he could louse them up, so I make a point of explaining to them, that whatever their problem is, they can overcome it by making it better. One such case was that of a woman with a load of dough who came to me on the advice of a person. Her problem was that her husband came home every night, with stolen furs, jewelry, diamonds and valuables, and tough friends, and when she asked him if this is what she could get out of her life with him, he lumped up her lip and head every night, as a sort of a bonus for not talking . . . 'cause if she did tell anyone, he said he'd kill her by gun, and do an equally like-wise thing to the person she told it to. I placed my forefinger gently over her mouth and pressed pretty good. I then said quickly, "Please don't say even what you just said! Can a man, who as you say, comes home every night, be all bad?"

Sometimes I tell people who have trouble about

too little money, and have a lot of kids, to get away from their problems, get a big dog, and a home in the country. There's nothing like luxury to make you forget how rotten it is to be a poor stupid slob with a lot of kids. I tell them how nice they'd feel with nothing to worry about. They could even have a maid and everything.

A lot of my rich friends tell me that, that way, poverty never seems to bother them. I myself love bird dogs, but they're very expensive. It costs a lot to buy them, and they don't have the healthiness of other real dogs. I took three of them on a country hike and threw them off a cliff. Not one of them could really fly.

A woman came into my office one afternoon, screaming and crying, and sat down and babbled dopily to me. She emptied her pocketbook on my desk, and while sobbing and choking up with sad feelings, pointed to a picture of our President on the wall. I said, "Madame, is something bothering you?" She said, "Yes, I'd like a drink of water." Wow, was I relieved, 'cause I realized then, lots of people get thirsty around that time of day.

I tell all my customers, "Husbands and wives wouldn't fight if they were happily married."

chapter seven?

PROBLEMS OF A REAL LEGAL LAWYER PERSON

I BELIEVE THERE is no short cut to learning, and when it comes to law things it is even harder. That's why I'm proud to say I've spent five and one-half hours of my whole life just learning all about law stuff. I guess ever since my very child-birth I have wanted to do something legal.

One of my first crook customers was a nice man who felt he had been tricked into sticking up thirty-two gas stations. The guys with him, tricked him by telling him he could get away with it. I knew after I heard what he did, that this man could end up in some sort of trouble.

As I stood in front of this man, talking to him, I knew at a glance, we were face to face. I wanted to say something to gain his confidence, so I said,

"I hear you're a big crook!" He punched me hard in the mouth. I knew then that he felt better. I chuckled through my swollen lips at how I had tricked him into relaxing. My whole face hurt me very much for seven weeks. Or thereabouts.

For two months, I planned my client's case out

very carefully. I surprised the judge and everybody. I got twenty-seven witnesses who identified my client as a crook. The judge person said he didn't know how a lawyer could do something like this to a client. I told him I worked nights on it.

Another man had been arrested while breaking into a bank vault, and was pretty much accused of it. His case was referred to me by a newspaper story I read about it. I went to the jail place and told him, as a lawyer, I felt he had nothing to worry about, if he could prove his innocence. He said his conscience wouldn't let him, and all he wanted me to do was get him a soft rap. I felt terrible, that that was all I could do for him, but that's all he wanted, so I got him a little fur jacket for his shoulders.

The only part of law studying I didn't get around to, was *starting.* I'm always open for a suggestion, and so I asked my best friend to please give me his opinion if I should become a great lawyer. He said truthfully he would rather not give an opinion. I pleaded with him as my best friend, I wanted his advice and what he thought I should do. He said, "Well personally, you have

to be crazy to go in for law at your age." I said,
"Oh yeah, what's it to you?"

The criminal in a case should always be re-
garded as the one on trial. If it's a murder trial,
or even something serious, and the judge tells
him he's going to get sort of electrocuted, the
lawyer should pep him up with a joke or two,
like go over and say, "Well, here's where your
insurance rate goes sky high." Or a sympathy
thing like, "It's all over in a few minutes or more,
and they cover up your head so nobody can see
if you're crying, so be a good sport like the rest
of us, and let's see that old smile, baby!"

Remember, it's up to the lawyer to make the
crook customer feel court is not too serious. I
myself, sometimes get up and play a little hand-
ball against the judge's big desk. It takes the
strain of the murder away. After I did that once,
a judge told me not to do it again, or I'd get arrested or something. I poked my murderer customer in the side and whispered, "Watch!" I did
it again, and got arrested, just to show the guy it
wasn't too serious.

Lawyers should know certain important things. Another lawyer can make you stop talking, by saying, "Objectionable" (which is "Shut up" in legal talk). Certain law words are just for lawyers and judges. Like, "You're disbarred," or "One more outburst . . ." "Clear the Court" and all that.

The judge wears a long black dress, in case someone dies. Always try to do smart things, like, don't bring in your client's murder weapon, even for a little joke.

Medicine-operating law is very different, and to go into a big judge court you have to really know it, and know it well, so I got another book.

A Mr. Ronald Fank came to me right after lunch, and he told me he had been to his doctor, who told him he needed to go for an appendix operation. He told his doctor, "Well, Doctor, you're the doctor!" and went for this appendix operation I just spoke of. Later during a talk with a nearby nurse, he found out from the nurse, that during the operation, they had removed his appendix from his entire body. He called a cop immediately, who said he could sue the hospital company for assault with a deadly weapon, and indecent exposure on an operating table while married nurses looked right at him.

I told him, that if this was all true, I felt he had a pretty good case. I am not one for snap judgment, and so I consulted with my hospital law expert assistant, who for seventeen years has been head elevator operator man at a very swell hospital. It was his unanimous opinion that my customer had a case, if he could prove he had never had these appendix taken out, or lost it kidding around, and also that he needed it for business.

We proved the first part somehow, but when

the judge heard how the scar made my suing customer embarrassed when he took a business client
to a Turkish bath, and the client looked right at
it, the judge asked how else they could have op-
erated. At this point I knew I had the judge reel-
ing. I told him, "They could have taken it out
from the inside."

Last month, a bunch of local citizens got together to try to get garbage picked up three times
a week, instead of semi-annually, you know, every
month. To handle this, they wanted someone who
really felt at home in garbage. I managed to make
them feel I was their man. I convinced them I
loved all garbage, not just cans, orange peels and
egg shells, but empty cartons, and crushed tooth-
paste tubes.

I had the committee over to my house for supper one night. By the time they left, they knew
I ate, drank, and slept garbage, and I'm sure they
sensed it was close to me. Some wisenheimer on
the committee tried to ease me out by saying I
wasn't fit to handle this city's garbage. At this
place in the talking, a quite polite lady with a tall

son named Fred, stood up and said, she knew of no one more fit to handle it than myself. I choked up a little at the thought of such confidence.

Soon I was named chairman, and from then on, from morning till night, no matter where I was, I had garbage on the tip of my tongue. I didn't quite succeed in improving the collections of garbage, but I did the very next best thing. I went around and collected all I could every Wednesday, Friday and Saturday, in the back seat of my new car.

chapter eight?

JUST YOUR HEALTH ALONE CAN TELL YOU IF YOU'RE WELL OR EVEN SICK

THE UNITED STATES Health Company in the Washington place is known for its decency in health stuff. They have a kind of nice little speech on the wall that holds up one side of the building. It says, "A man's body means as much to him, as any other part of him." This is more than just a important motto saying.

What has science done for us over the past eight and a half or nine and a half years? Well, nowadays nobody need be afraid of dentists any more 'cause, most of them are young guys, and not scary-looking any more. Also now, vitamin pills help keep you in shape to visit your doctor.

A woman came to me and asked what I thought made her so heavy. I said: "If I may speak to you like a person, I think it's your weight." She said, "You're kidding, aren't you?"

I said, "Lady, this is a business store, not a comedy place."

I have certain rules for health. They include all the things I have in my rules, and if you don't stick to them, it will be like going ahead and not doing what I have in these rules.

I have found that there is a crying need for specialists who know about hair that grows out of the skin. A woman who had a full-grown heavy beard, asked me if I thought it could be hormones. I told her, "No, it was just hair." I went on to comfort her. I said, "There is nothing to be ashamed of. There are many like you who have beards, and they have gone on to become famous wealthy men. Now you can't say as much for beardless women."

Height has been a problem of people ever since modern times, and the invention of the tape measure. A father and mother of a real child, came to me recently, and they were both rather short as far as their height was concerned. They asked what I thought would be the best thing for their son to do to assure his being taller than they. I told them the best thing for him to do, would be to grow much taller than them. In that way, he would avoid two problems. One: what to do about being too short, and secondly another problem, about something.

I've had so many requests from so many people who have never been any taller than their full grown height, that I published a book which is of interest to people of every height from four feet to six feet. Each page is a picture of a person a quarter of an inch taller than the one before. It's called, "A Book of Pictures of Folks Four Feet to Six Feet Tall."

A woman came to me with her seventeen-year-old daughter, who was losing her teeth. I placed her on a special diet. She was not to eat food at mealtimes, and follow it with a full glass of vinegar immediately. I had seen this system work really wonderful on pack rats at the 1939 World's Fair. Three weeks later she came back to my office with a cop, and told me her daughter had lost all her hair, and that her skin looked all tarnished, and puffed-up in little balls. I told her if she was going to pay attention to silly little side-effects, I'd have to drop her case, because I felt she didn't have any confidence in me.

A woman who had never been to a doctor since immediately after she was born, came to me and said she'd been sick all her life, what could she do to get her health back? I sat her down and told her a little story about a friend of mine who got a traffic ticket.

I receive a lot of letters by mail, asking me, does food have anything to do with gaining weight? I feel, "Only if you swallow it. And then, of course, only if you get fat from it."

The President, himself an actual eater of food, told me he and the missus quite often sit down to a meal. I asked the President if he had a favorite dish. He said, yes, he did. Then I asked him how old he was. I had a good reason for asking him this. I wanted to find out his age.

I myself, first became interested in food, as a child. My mother used to serve us some, along with what she cooked us to eat.

During a very swell testing thing we did on living people, we fed a special breakfast cereal to a young man for twenty-seven days, and we noticed a wonderful change. His skin, his hair, and yes, even his nails, turned to brilliant feathers. In three months from the testing start, he flew away.

Sports and general exercise are lots of good. Soccer builds up resistance to dandruff, and really helps save you money. Like after you get lumps on your head from the bouncing of the soccer ball off your head for years, and they operate on you, shaving your head for the operation, cleans off any loose dandruff flakes, and like I said, saves you money, by your not having to buy a clothes brush for your suit, which is no small item.

Very deadly poisons can prove harmful, if taken by the body or mouth. More on this a little later on when I feel like writing about it.

Horse racing is great exercise for the nose. It clears up clogged nose holes for the best jockey. When he wins the race, a man comes and puts a lot of flowers over the horse, and the jockey breathes the smell of them in, and makes his head feel all empty again.

I think skin diving is too dangerous. I prefer to dive taking along my whole body. You know, the bones, blood vessels, hair, and all that. The entire equipment needed for skin diving, isn't cheap by any means. It is expensive by these means, I just spoke of. You must first of all buy the basic needs, like a whole breathing thing. It has a hose and a box with a whole breath of air in it. It has a mouthpiece, which you stick in your own mouthpiece, and which you continue to breathe real air through. When you've been down too long, the air stuff in the big can, lets you know by a special signal. The signal is, you can't breathe, and you feel sick about it. This automatically sends a message to your brain to try to look around for some air some place up on top of the water.

I get all kinds of screwy health things people want to know about. One woman asked what she could do for a recurring earache. I told her to do a lot of deep sea diving because it's the best thing I know of for a good earache, if that's what she likes.

Now and then we become worried about something we may be thinking about, and we sort of forget that worry itself can make you think of sad things. You should have a little laugh, a little joy, and even something pleasant. That way, you can feel happy when worries are on your mind. A lot of folks ask me if diet has anything to do with what we eat.

I tell them all the same thing.

Now as to the amount of vitamins in our food. Today a lot of food is eaten for internal use, with the remainder being used for human consumption. That in itself is what I've said.

As a matter of fact, I have just unproved the idea, that certain foods are good for different bodily parts. I made a thorough study of this in a good science place. I found brain food is greatly exaggerated. I fed one man special brain food for his brain, for a week, and the brain absorbed none of it. In fact it made such a mess of his hair, I had to shampoo him every night. Next we come to all that bull about good food for bloodbuilding. May I tell you, I know good food, and I poured a whole pot of really swell soup on a spot where a man had just been recently shot. I hung around and kept looking at it a lot . . . I might as well have poured some cheap food on the bullet place for all the good it did. It honestly didn't even build one blood.

A lot of badness of health is based on a person's physical condition. For three years I was manager of a health saloon. We had dumbbells, weight pulleys, medicine balls, a shower and a towel. Everything was under very much supervision. Nobody was ever allowed to leave with the towel. One chap, who was a strapping six-foot two inches, and weighed just over 126 pounds, came to my very attention, and said he had been suffering from shortness of breath, and little severe pains in his chest. He said his doctor told him it was all mental. He said he wanted some good exercise to help get himself out of his mind. I put this chap on the weight pulleys for sixteen straight hours. I made him stop it when he kept passing out near the end, lest he get his foot caught in them, and hurt himself. I told him to run over to the shower, and cool off with a real cold shower, and lie down for a minute in the fan room. While laying down, he must have allowed those little severe chest pains to come back into the mental part of his mind, because we had to refund the money to his widow. I just thank goodness he didn't get hurt while under my watching.

You must train children properly in health things. They are, after all, only young, and not too smart about much stuff. If we find they are not doing health things good, we should punish them,

by depriving them of the things they want most,
like air and water. My two own children Mar-
garet, and his older brother Mary Ellen, 27 and 27
and a half years each, respectfully, know that if
they don't get to bed on time, I won't tell them
where elephants go to die, when they reach the
age of thirty years old. This almost kills them.

Some people in the prime of life, find that poor
health can louse up a marriage. A wife and husband came to me and told me they were going to
get a divorce, that she was sick from his actions.
I told them I hated to see that happen to them,
because in each case of a similar nature divorce
usually seemed to ruin the marriage. I told them
that if they wanted a divorce, they might as well
separate for good. Anything is better than breaking up a home. I asked her, (that's the person
who's the wife), if she believed in childbirth, feeling that maybe her body might be missing some
rather important parts. She smiled, and said, that
wasn't her problem. I smiled right back a little
bit, and told her I understood, because I myself
was born.

I said to her to tell me if there was anything
troubling them, and she said a story to me about
his going out every night, and that he had had five

children with other women since their marriage, and that this had caused her some upsetness. I told her if she was going to beat around the bush, and not tell me what was causing the trouble between them, I couldn't help them.

Then the gentleman, (who was the husband of them), got up on his high horse, and said I was a nut. I winked at her and said right in front of both of them, so he could hear me too: "I guess a lot of things happen at City Hall, that you don't know about out in the country." I winked at her again, as though what I said meant something. Then I turned to him and asked: "Did you ever think of all the joy that happiness could bring you?"

I said, in continuing my talking, "Furthermore, this wouldn't happen, if you were happily married."

Nerves in your body should be in good working order, so you could take stress and strains, if you happen to be involved in everyday living. Sometimes, a pet can make you feel not even nervous. Animals make the best kind of pets. They will listen to whatever you tell them, and many of the ones I have seen, have just as much brains as I have. You can tell them things, and they will listen to you tell them those very things. I shall never forget the look on my brother's face, when

I came home with my first dog. I asked my friend's father who was a retired dog-doctor since he lost his license, what kind of a dog it was. He said it was a rabid dog. I felt so proud, because I was the only one in the neighborhood who had one.

Cleanliness helps you from being sick just as

much as you could possibly think. Dishes, especially the very ones you eat out of, should be washed. Also, your own body should be washed. Not in the dish water mind you, but later, after you go upstairs to the bathroom. A little dirt on your body can make germs grow right up. You should take a bath every once in a while, and let that water upstairs in the bathroom I spoke of, wash the dirt away, right while you're in there. I cannot talk important enough about the washing business, because, as the Latins say, "Cleanliness is really swell!"

Finally, stay away from any dread contagious diseases if they are of the serious kind. That way, it will help you keep better without going to the doctor and getting a needle with a wonder drug right inside of it.

THE DIVESTMENT COUNSELOR

As a man who tells people how to do things with their money, I must say that too many people worry about making the wrong kind of investments. I personally am quite contrary. I don't care what they do with their money. Many millionaires, who themselves are notoriously well-to-do, have asked me if I could run their wealth into a fortune.

You see, I became an expert financial wizard, quite by chance. I invested my mother's entire savings which she had even accrued, in a venture I had received a tip on, and which I had great confidence in. The name of the particular stock was, "The Great Atlantic Tunnel." I was told about it by a nice man with glasses, who was talking to another fine-looking man about the new proposed Atlantic Bridge. He advised me to get in quick, before the "Smarties" get in. He whispered to me that the tunnel would be ready long before they even started to build the bridge. I thereupon gave him all my mother's money, and choked back a little laugh I had in me, for his taking me for a sucker. I then pardoned myself, and went home and got my father's life savings, and bought the "bridge" stock from the other nice gentleman. I've always believed in playing it safe.

There are several kinds of investments—some for short term, some for long term, some for capital gains, and some just to make money. These latter investments are called, "Lucky."

A very well known financial-type banker and gentleman, came into my office just a short little time ago. He said he had some very important news to tell me. I told him, if he didn't object, I had more important things to do, and slammed the door in his face. Or, anyway, near his face.

A woman, who had been making a lot of money in the hands of a big stock investor, heard about me through someone's talking, and was curious if I could do better for her. Well, may I tell you, in three months, I had her whole fortune, lost, and in one way, she felt better. She wasn't curious anymore. I felt that at least this way she knew where it all went, which was not like wasting it, I told her.

Another woman, a Mrs. Hulot Harbinger, who shall remain nameless, had a similar experience. She was permanently sick since birth from a sort of illness. Now, at eighty-eight years old, she had fifty-two hundred dollars saved and invested in some silly thing or other that was bringing in an income.

I told her to think of the future, think and plan for her old age, and invest in something tangible for a bundle she could have for later in life. Well, she did, and inside of six months she called up to check on it. I told her I was pleased to tell her that she had lost every cent she had in the world. I was pleased, because I had the strength to tell her the truth, and I feel that truth is a big part of character. She hung up and came over to my office, all upset about something. I told her it was bad enough she lost all that lifelong savings money, let alone to let it upset her. Then I sat her down, and gave her some sensible advice. I said, "All this can make you feel terrible for the whole day, so why not forget it, like me?"

She mumbled incoherently, "You advised me! You advised me!"

I patted her shoulder, and said, "Go listen to people!" Seeing she was sort of shook up about being dead broke, I used psychology and told her that this whole thing could affect her heart.

You see, I specialize in catering to the old and the confirmed. Another request I often get from many many people I advise, is not to invest all their money in one kind of stock—losers.

A lot of folks and even people of other races, come and tell me they worry about money. Especially people with financial problems. I have a advice talk I tell those who ask about what they should do with this money, of which they're worrying about. I advise young people to prepare now for their future, like buy a couple of swell cemetery plots for their old age. Actually, you don't have to use them until you're ready. In the meantime, you know you've got something to look forward to. It's like having a present in the closet, and you can't open it until you're dead.

A man in my profession owes a great debt to people in many other fields. The man to whom I am referring is Dr. George C. Perch. He owes eight hundred dollars on his car, three hundred dollars on his wife's teeth repairing, one hundred

and ten dollars on his television set. But wait, I
shouldn't even be telling this much, let alone
what I've just said. You'll probably think me a
chattering box, but he does owe it, and plenty
more which I could tell you about.

A gentleman customer asked me if he should
take out a health and accident policy with some
money he had left over from an investment he
made through me. I told him I thought that was
darn swell. I told him I'd get it for him. He hes-
itated, recalling our recent poor good luck. I told
him I could get him a policy, where they wouldn't
even ask if he was alive, let alone examine him. He
thought that was good enough. I sent him over to
my friend, and he got the policy.

Three weeks later, he called me to come to the
hospital where he seemed to be living since a
somewhat serious heart and brain operation. He
said it came on suddenly and he needed to collect.
I checked and found out that the company didn't
like cry-baby people, and that he would have to
collect on the point system. The company felt
that if you were well enough to point a finger at
anything, you were considered just trying to act
very rotten. I told him, however, the company
wouldn't arrest him or anything for trying to col-

lect. They just kid around about it like it was a misunderstanding of the contract, and let it go by having a representative visit his house, and yell at his wife, that they were cheap lousy chislers or something, and then they forget it. That's why it pays to deal with a reputable firm.

An older man of seventy-eight years old, who had scrimped and saved three thousand two hundred dollars through delivering messages and things for over fifty-six years, and had deprived himself of even little luxuries, had heard about my plan, and had me invest his money for him in a certain thing . . . Inside of two weeks he came running to me with an article in the paper, that the company was bankrupt. I read it and complimented him on being very observant. This kind of thing makes people feel nice . . . He then said, he didn't dare let himself think about all his savings being lost. I said, "That's the way to face it—easy come, easy go!"

I've had letters from bankers, heads of investment institutions, and even respectable citizens have called me time and time again, but I'm still in business anyway.

DOING THE GOVERNMENT LAW
JOBS IS PLENTY OF DARN WORK

As I TOLD the guys in the Congressman place, during speeching one time, I said, "We were put in
this government Congress job, by people who expect us to do good law stuff for them. So let's do
good law jobs for these friends who put us in this
soft job, and forget about what the voters want.
Always remember the famous words of Thomas
Jefferson, 'cause he said, some really swell words,
when he was in this business."

Just this morning, my secretary told me something I never knew before.

Another thing I am often asked along with questions, is whether I believe in picking a favorite son at the convention. I say to this, "No, because, you see, I have two, and one of them would get jealous. Probably the older one, Betty Ann."

The President asked me what I thought about our new space program. I said, "Your Highness, sir, I think it's great. I saw it twice, once on channel four. It's a lot of laughs." Then he asked me what I thought about people traveling in space. I told him I thought it was the most comfortable way. It's certainly better than traveling all cramped up.

Every day we spend so much time in the government room talking about bills different people send in, we don't get to do no legal stuff. People should pay their bills themselves, instead of making us guys in the government building waste our valuable leisure time.

At a recent debate on our country's little bit of water supply, I listened for as long as I could without speaking up. Finally I could contain myself for no longer a period of time. I requested by asking, if I could speak on this very subject by voice. The man with the hammer said, "Yes, you can. But only like for a few minutes." I said, "Fel-

low gentlemen, you got your brains in your nose."
It was just a fragment of speech for a little joke
but it hit home. I continued speaking on. "Right
to the south of our entire National ground, we've
got a whole normal reservoir. I'm referring to the
Gulf of Mexico—as this normal reservoir of which
I'm speaking. Just looking on any map any dope
can see it's like in a big round pot, and deep as
anything, I bet. And it's all ours except for a little
bit of the water that floats right next to that
Mexico country. You don't even need to say anything to them about it. How, you inquire? Simple.
Some night, just dump a whole ton of sand at the
place across the bottom of the map, where it's
open, and drips out to South America.

"After we use up the water in several weeks,
make a little hole in that sand I told you to dump
in, and let it fill up from that water that floats up
every day from South America."

When you're just a plain voter every day, like
I was for years, you don't really appreciate
amendments and that kind of uppity stuff. After
I became a Congress, I learned it's not all peaches

and cream, with a little sugar but not too much please. In running for public office, a lot of people don't realize three very important facts, and they really ought to.

Ever since I was legally elected, I never knew why there was only a certain number of guys in Congress, until one day I asked a fellow worker, while he wasn't busy, and he explained that the reason was, that there was just enough chairs, and you couldn't stand, according to the fire laws. Another amazing thing was that you could find people here from every state in the bunch.

Newspaper reporters ask you certain things which you must be ready to answer with a reply. For instance, they asked me what I thought about foreign aid one day. They said, "How are you going to vote on the foreign aid?" I said, without a minute of waiting time, "Are you kidding?" You see, they like a man who sticks his neck out on an issue.

At a closed door meeting on road building, I opened it to get some air. They asked me if I had anything else to contribute. I said, "Yes, I did." I told the whole gang in the room, this:

"What do you think America is, some little tiny city, in some nearby hick town? America is an entire whole big place, and that's why you can't just drive around the corner if you want to go on a long trip. If you're going to enjoy driving on our country's roads, you should make it your business to go by car. And likewise it is our nice duty to see that roads are placed at strategic intervals."

"Bottlenecks are a rotten problem at best. And they always happen at very busy places. This can be easily and cheaply changed. How? By simply putting up wrong direction signs, right in front of that place where the bottleneck is. Then, when the people who followed the goofy signs get back on the right road, it'll be all cleared up. I think this much is expected of us by those people who are members of America, and who ride inside their car while going through this wonderful ground we're in. And always remember, no matter where you go in this whole America thing, from Maine to California, or even from coast to coast, you must get there by traveling."

Just then one of the men looked at me, and asked me to see if the door locked from the outside. I guess it was for safety precaution, I guess. I pardoned myself from speeching, and went out and tried it. It locked! But apparently they didn't hear my knocking for two hours to get back in to speak some more—so I left.

In traveling abroad through this country, I have found that there is more Americanism in this country, than any other country. Each state I visited, was a different one, and each one had certain special things about it. The spelling of the names alone, were different than each other.

Each state had its special favorite flower. I had to wear it in each state. However, my own favorite flower is a bouquet, but only as a first choice. The President's favorite flower is the one he likes best, and yet I always see him wearing another one.

On a recent visit to this country from a foreign land of his, a very swell king came here to visit around and I was on the table committee. I of course was asked to prepare a flower thing around the table. I found out through a secret way, that the king's favorite flower was the American beauty rose. Knowing that even kings love surprises, I went ahead and set up five thousand marigolds and was he surprised!

A friend of mine was going to England to purchase some rare flowers. I asked him if I could borrow his spade while he was away. He said, "Certainly," and gave it to me.

As I have said before, you must always be ready to answer questions about anything. I remember one time, just last night, I appeared on a television show, and some kid asked me what I thought about Alaska. I answered him right on the spot. I said, "I think it's way up north, if you'd like to know." You've got to be quick and accurate, or they'll make you look like a jerk on the television.

Speaking of kids, let us take education for a minute. Let us go back hundreds of years, all through history. We find that all through those hundreds of years I just mentioned, people looked sort of dopey in pictures, because of the clothes they put on to wear. However, those same people are never seen alive, so why should we embarrass them by putting their pictures in history books, wearing dopey old time clothes, for kids to laugh at? But if we do put them in books while still wearing those old time ago clothes, let's try to make it like it was a mistake, or was put in the book by some guy fooling around. Like say, if it's Columbus crossing the Delaware in an old-fashioned suit, it should say on the botton of the whole picture: "This is Columbus crossing the Delaware in an old-time Italian suit, 'cause he was going to a stupid masquerade party in it when he got over here." (And have an arrow, or maybe a drawing of a finger, pointing to an opposite side from where he was driving from.)

As a Congress person, or even Senately speaking, you get some crazy requests for helping other people, other than yourself. Late one time when it was Friday, a lady from her own home town, came into my office with a very nice face, and three children of hers, and asked if I thought she should get married. I looked at her, and the three kids, and said, "Boy, this is a great time to ask a question like that, at six o'clock on a Friday." I continued, "Aren't you ashamed of yourself? These kids will miss their supper."

chapter
eleven?

THE THINGS A JUNGLE HUNTER NEEDS TO GO HUNTING IN THE JUNGLE

SAFARI, WHICH I should explain in every-day talk, means a whole bunch of guys going into the jungle to look for something.

The first big game we saw, when we went, was a large HORSE! I was told not to shoot it, because it was carrying all our stuff. Lesson number one, don't shoot your pack horse!

A very sad thing happened to one of our party on our third day out. That must happen a lot out there.

The rhinoceros is a very strange type of ani-mule. If you shoot him nine or ten or eleven times, with a great big kind of bullet, and he isn't really dead yet, he seems to sense through instinct, that he's hurt. At that time, it is best not to go and pet him, like if you want to say you're sorry.

The elephant, which is as strong as anything, has two tusks, which are stuck right in his head. The best way to describe him, is like when they say someone is as big as an elephant, they mean

this animal. Although they have a terrible temper, not one ever got sore at me and tried to—you know—give me the business.

A friend of mine on the Safari, by the name of Frank Thomas, was kaneeling down to shoot at a sore-headed lion who was charging down on him. I yelled, "Hey look what's on your back Boobie," just for laughs! To this day, I can't seem to explain my silly little horseplay to his widow.

A word of advice for you kids just kidding around in the jungle for the first time. Never turn your back and try to, well, try to just ignore a wild charging beast. He could really jump up on you and tear your coat or shirt, even.

Hunting, not just like hunting rabbits or wild squirrel but I mean real big adult people's hunting, is no joke. You've got to plan it. You have to get a lot of stuff together for jungle hunting. You've got to be prepared for any unforeseen emergency, and things you don't even expect. Safety and medicine things are always in great requirement. First of all, you have to have a bandage, because you could sure stick yourself on a thornlike bush or other wild berry plant. And that's only part of the danger out there. Another danger lies in the swamps. You could slip in an alligator-filled swamp at night and catch a cold. That's where it pays to possess a box of tissues to sneeze into. A little care now might save spreading your cold around to the gunbearers or someone else, even.

Then too, you have to know the way various animals do their things. Some of them are pretty smart, while others seem to know *exactly* what they're doing. I have found that many of the animals have a brain like my very own, but of course that's only by comparison, and then too, I can't do things as perfectly as they do, so it isn't fair.

Even an expert can make a mistake in judging things out in the jungle there. Like a sudden shift in the wind, can make the hunting stop right away. For one thing, this makes the animal you want to shoot at, know you're hanging around from the way you smell, even if you took a bath just maybe an hour or even twenty minutes ago. And if that did happen, he could logically run right up to you and bite your whole body up.

The elephant is a conceited animal, and doesn't know when to cut it out. One day we came upon a whole bunch of these stocky creatures, and I didn't know you should be quiet. Kiddingly I yelled, "Hey, Fatso!" Well, in two seconds there was elephants all over, trumpeting loud as hell. I only meant it as a little joke, but somehow one of them took offense, and passed the word around. Gee!

You should not overlook having a walking-stick, made out of wood. You could either buy one when you leave your house in America, or break one off a tree when you get to Africa. You can use it like a cane, and look like a fancy English hunter, or use it once in a while to go up to a native luggage carrier and tap him on the shoulder with it saying, "Good job," or other such comments.

The water problem in the jungle isn't too good either. You could be taking a little walk deep in the jungle sometime, and get terrifically thirsty, and the only water in sight might be in a hidden water-hole. When you go to take a little drink from it, you find it tastes like poison. So take smart precautions. Take a drink before you leave your jungle house, then if you get thirsty later, stop off some place for a cold drink.

Not to be forgotten, is the trapping things for bringing the wild animals back. If you're going to take them alive, you need at least four hundred feet of string and some cartons.

Sentiment plays its part in "The Hunt," so let us not overlook taking with us two very important things—a paper and a pencil to write down the names and addresses of native-folk people on the safari, to write to when the hunting is through. A pen pal is worth over twelve hundred and fifty dollars—and even more when you're home on those lonely nights with just your friends and loved ones.

Now we are ready to get under the way. A checker goes over our list of things I just outlined, and we double-check them, just to make sure that the first time we checked them, they are the same as the double time we checked them secondly. A whistle blows, and someone says, "Safari Pawana Gooa toku." This is sort of like Simon Says, with animals, 'cause when he says these words, all of us get in line at once and prepare to take off. The Bawaia Kutu, who is the head of the whole gang of us, comes up to each one of us and asks us if we have our salt pills, and we say "Yes" if we have them and "No" if we don't have them. And those who say "Yes" he allows to board the truck to the jungle limits, and those who say they don't have their salt pills are also allowed to get on the truck, because the Bawaia Kutu doesn't give a damn whether you have them or not. In just a matter of time, it will be "Ralla peto Kuwa Sima Sima Bondo Loo Atiena!", six-thirty.

Telegram blanks, by the way, should be carried at all times, for humor has its proper place in the hunting business. If someone or other is severely injured by a very very wild animal attack on him, and he has to lie down in his tent and can't be moved before help arrives, you can send him gag telegrams, which he really doesn't have to answer. "Plane with blood plasma for victim lost landing gear, and can't land. Have to send messenger with it on foot 500 miles." Another form gag message is, "Cannot possibly get proper wonder drug and other medicine things to you in time. Bon Voyage!"

And last but not least of all, remember to take a measuring string to find out how long an animal is from head to tip, or actually where his tail joins his body. This will give you an idea of his length, and you can write it down on the back of that piece of paper I told you to take, to write the names of the people you want to write to, when you get back home on those lonely nights.

So as we say in the jungle, "Let's get started hunting some animals."

THE END?